The Canoe Maker

David Moses Bridges,
Passamaquoddy Birch Bark Artisan

WRITTEN BY Jean Flahive & Donald Soctomah

ILLUSTRATED BY Mari Dieumegard

Designed and produced by:
Maine Authors Publishing
12 High Street, Thomaston, Maine 04861
www.maineauthorspublishing.com

Printed in the United States of America

Dedications

To Tobias, Sabattus, and Natanis. May the words of your father pass into your hearts.

—*Jean Flahive*

To our ancestors, and to future generations of birch bark tribal artisans. David carried on ancestral birch bark traditions and, during his life, passed them on to other generations so the traditions would continue. The white birch is one of the most important trees for the Passamaquoddy people, and its bark is deeply interwoven into our history and our lives. The bark was used in constructing wigwams where people were born and spent days and nights with family. Birch bark is also used in basket making, calling moose, and to travel the rivers and ocean in canoes. In the olden days the birch bark served as a vessel to carry people to the spirit world.

—*Donald Soctomah*

To Jeff: Thank you for joining me in our canoe as we paddle through life.

And to those who knew and loved David, I hope my artwork captures and honors his creative spirit.

—*Mari Dieumegard*

Reader's Note: To help you pronounce the Native American words used in our story, please refer to the pronunciation key on the last page of the book.

A June dawn splashed over Passamaquoddy Bay. David Moses Bridges and his nine year-old son Tobias left their tribal home and set out for the forest in the eastern hills of Maine. Tobias wiggled with excitement. His father was a master canoe maker in their tribe, and he was going to teach Tobias how to build a birch bark canoe just like their ancestors did.

"Building a birch bark canoe begins in the forest," David said as he led his son down a little-known trail. "All the materials we need will be found here. We call this part, and what we get, our 'gatherings'."

They walked among the tall red and white pines, grey-barked maples, and oak trees, passing through stands of slender snow-colored birches bending gracefully to reach the sun.

"Dad, why do you build birch bark canoes?" asked Tobias, eager and curious about his new adventure.

"When I was little, my great-grandfather Sylvester Gabriel told me stories from the Old Time. For more than a thousand years the Passamaquoddy people built canoes to travel the open ocean and go into the great forests by using the lakes and rivers. Great-grandfather built his canoes the same way our ancestors did, from the winter bark of the white birch. I wanted to make my own canoe with him, but he died before he could teach me."

"Who taught your great-grandfather how to make a canoe?"

"Probably his grandpa or his dad. Our people pass on our ways by telling stories to the children, who then pass the stories on to their children. Great-grandfather learned to build a canoe from the stories that were told to him."

"But if he died, how did he pass it on to you?"

"He passed it into my heart. His stories guided me to a master canoe maker, Steve Cayard, who builds canoes in the traditional way. I learned from him, but my great-grandfather's tools guide me, too." David stopped, opened his pouch and showed Tobias a crooked knife, a barking knife, a drawknife, awl and an axe. "When I hold his tools in my hands, I feel a deep connection with the past. I believe the work that I do is not mine alone. It is a creation of the land and our people."

They hiked deep into the forest. Each time David spotted a tall and thick white birch, he stopped and studied it. And each time, he would shake his head in disappointment and walk away. They searched for most of the day. No perfect birch tree was found.

As darkness settled in the forest, David and Tobias made camp. They rolled out their sleeping bags near a pond, its dark waters peppered with lily pads. David collected a number of large rocks and placed them in a circle on the forest floor. "We call the rocks 'grandfathers'," he said. "Like our elders, they take care of us and the world around us. This circle of rocks will keep the flames that warm us within its bounds and protect the forest, too."

David and Tobias ate a meal of dried moose meat and pine-needle tea warmed from the campfire as they watched the silvery-white moon rise high in the sky. Soon it was time to crawl into their sleeping bags.

"Tell me a story," pleaded Tobias.

David stared at the star-studded sky. "There is an old story of the first canoe. Many Indians believe the *mociyehs*, the partridge, was the first great canoe maker."

"A partridge?" Tobias was astonished.

David spoke softly. "If you are quiet in the woods, you might hear a partridge pecking, *thump, thump*, at a hollow log hidden in the low bush. In the Old Time, the partridge was the canoe maker for the birds of the forest. He made a canoe for *cihpolakon*—that means eagle—and the *cihpolakon* used the ends of his wings as paddles. He made a canoe for *kuhkukhahs*, the owl, and *kasq*, the crane, and *tihtiyas*, the blue jay. And for the hummingbird, *alamossit*, he made a little boat, with tiny paddles. But then the other birds asked the partridge why he had not built a canoe for himself. The partridge hinted that the canoe he was building would be a wonder such as the birds had never seen. The partridge thumped busily for many days."

CIHPOLAKON

KUHKUKHAHS

TIHTIYAS

ALAMOSSIT

KASQ

"At last the day came and all the birds gathered on the banks to see the partridge's new canoe. The partridge had reasoned that if a canoe having two ends could be paddled in two directions, then a boat that was round, could be paddled in any direction! So he had made his canoe as round as a bird's nest. His feathered friends were astonished that this simple idea had not occurred to any of them.

The proud partridge slid his round canoe into the water and started to paddle, but the small boat simply turned round and round in endless circles. The humbled partridge finally made it ashore, flew far into the forestland and hid himself in shame under the low bushes where he remains today."

David whispered. "When you hear a *thump, thump* it may be the partridge still pecking, building a wondrous canoe."

Tobias burrowed deeper into his sleeping bag. Around the pond, spring peepers sounded like a thousand tiny bells, and a bull frog croaked in the cool water. He thought he heard a faint *thump, thump* from the underbrush, but he was so sleepy he closed his eyes and dreamed of the sad little partridge and his round canoe.

The next morning father and son hiked along the banks of a lake. At last David shouted, "Over there! Perhaps it will be the perfect birch for our canoe!"

The magnificent birch stood tall and straight. David wrapped his arms around its thick trunk. "The tree is wide enough. The bark is mostly smooth and it's good there are few branches."

David climbed mid-way up the birch tree. He took out his great-grandfather's barking knife and sliced into its bark. He called down to Tobias. "There are two layers; the outer bark which is white, and the inner bark which is brownish-red. The inner layer feeds the tree, so I take only the outer bark. That way the tree may go on living."

David slid down the tree and held a piece of bark in his hand. He showed it to Tobias. "If the bark doesn't crack when I twist it, it will be the right thickness to make a canoe."

He twisted the bark but it did not crack. They smiled at each other. They had found the perfect birch tree.

This time David climbed to the top and made a crosswise cut into the bark all around the tree. Then he made two more cuts, one at the middle and one at the base of the tree. Finally he made one long cut, lengthwise, from the top to the bottom of the tree. The cuts allowed them to lift the bark away from the tree and roll it into one large piece.

"We must say a prayer of thanks to the tree's spirit," David told his son. "Thank you, Creator, for providing us with this bark that will make a good and strong canoe." Taking out a leather pouch of sage and native tobacco, David emptied some at the base of the tree. "The birch has given us the gift of its bark, so I leave a gift in return. These are medicinal plants that will help the tree heal."

They carried the roll of birch bark back to their camp.

The next morning they tramped further into the woods to where the cedar trees were numerous. Using his great-grandfather's axe, David chopped down a cedar tree. He explained to Tobias that the cedar would be cut into planks and used for the gunwales and the ribs of the canoe.

On the following day, they set out to gather spruce roots. They found a stand of spruce trees where the earth was sandy and loamy, making it easier to gather the roots. Together they pulled and pulled great lengths of roots. "We'll split the roots and use them like thread to stitch the bark to the ribs of the canoe."

David pointed to several thick masses on the trunk of one of the spruce trees. "This is the tree's sap," he told his son. "We call it spruce gum. When a tree is injured, the gum oozes out and dries into a hard mass around the wound. It keeps diseases and bugs from burrowing inside the tree while it's healing." He instructed Tobias to use a stick to scrape the gum from the trunk.

"What's the spruce gum used for?" asked Tobias as he poked away at the hardened gum, chipping it off in clumps and dropping it into a basket. His nostrils filled with the gum's strong smell.

"We use it to seal the canoe's seams to make it water tight."

It was their last night at camp, David looked at all they had collected. "We've finished our gatherings. The forest has given us many gifts. Gathering the right materials is essential in building a birch bark canoe," David explained. "It's why I wanted you to come with me. Gathering materials using the way of our ancestors is a tradition that needs to be passed on to you."

Back at home, David and Tobias began to build the canoe. He told his son the work would be very slow and will take many weeks.

Using great-grandfather's drawing knife, they split the cedar along the wood's grain, and smoothed it with the crooked knife as they carved the cedar into slender planks of varying lengths. The planks were soaked in water for several days and then placed in boiling water, which made the cedar flexible enough to bend and form the boat's gunwales—the boat's upper edges—and the ribs.

Days later, David placed a gunwale frame he made on the unrolled bark, and weighted it down with rocks. Then the bark was raised to form the sides of the canoe and held in place with stakes. With great-grandfather's awl, David punched holes in the bark. The spruce roots were passed through the holes and laced around the gunwales. It was a long and tiring process lacing and stitching all the bark, making sure everything was held tightly together.

At last, the stitching was completed, but the canoe was very loose and bendable. It was time for the cedar planks. David told Tobias that the thin planks were called sheathing and would be placed on the inside of the canoe to give it more strength. But to give the canoe its final shape and to hold the sheathing, David showed Tobias how to fit the cedar ribs under the gunwales and drive them all into place.

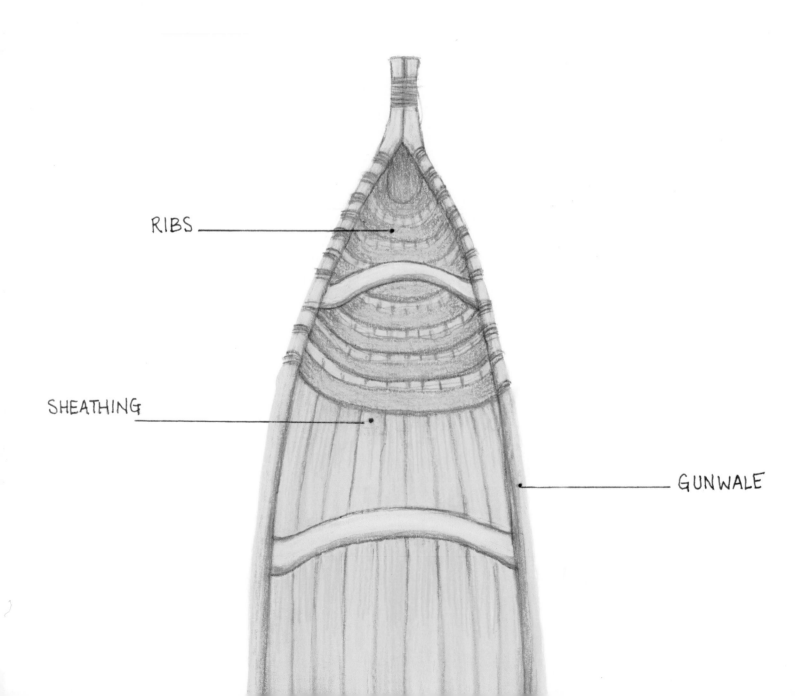

RIBS

SHEATHING

GUNWALE

Finally, David took the raw spruce gum Tobias had gathered, placed it all in an old pot mixed with ash and bear fat, and cooked it slowly until the lumps turned into thick, amber liquid. He showed Tobias how to apply it to all the seams where the bark had been sewn together. It was very sticky, and Tobias worked quickly to spread the spruce gum evenly over the seams.

By summer's end, their canoe could finally be launched. David and Tobias headed for a cove on Passamaquoddy land, carrying the canoe along a narrow path through tangled low bush.

Thump, thump!

They stopped and listened again for the muffled sound.

Thump, thump!

"It's the partridge!" Tobias whispered. "I know it is!"

David nodded. They set the canoe down and waited.

Mociyehs emerged from the low bush and stared at the canoe. Then it inched closer. Bobbing its head up and down, the partridge circled the canoe, pecking at it here and there. Finally the quick little bird scurried away into the bush.

David and Tobias listened for several moments.

There was no *thump, thump*.

"Perhaps the little partridge thinks a wondrous canoe has been built at last, and he is happier now," David said.

On the pebbled shore rested an old and tattered birch bark canoe. Peels of bark had lifted and rippled in the salty sea air. They set their canoe down beside it.

"There is one more lesson," David said. "We believe that the spirit from the old canoe must pass to the new one to protect it."

He pulled a handful of sage from his pouch. Scattering the sage across the bow of the old canoe and holding an eagle feather, David offered an ancient blessing. He lit the remaining sage and placed the leaves in a large seashell. A sweet-smelling smoke engulfed the canoes. Then he took his son's hand and told him to stand quietly.

Moments passed. They watched a fishing eagle swoop low, hover over the close blue sea, and then soar into the inlet forest.

A lone cloud drifted lazily across the sky and lingered over the old canoe, casting a shadow across its bow. The shadow swirled in the sudden breeze and for a moment, David thought he saw the silhouette of his great-grandfather. The shadow lifted from the old bow, floated, and disappeared into the new canoe. David glanced at the sky. The spirit cloud was gone.

Turning to Tobias, David said, "The spirit will protect our canoe. I learned to build a birch bark canoe in the way of our ancestors. But passing these traditions on to you is my real work. Too much of our Native American culture is fading. It is important to recognize our uniqueness and our connection to the past and future. One day, Tobias, Great-grandfather's tools will be yours. Already, some of his stories are yours, to care for, and to share someday, with your children and siblings."

David and Tobias climbed into their birch bark canoe and paddled into the splendor of Passamaquoddy Bay.

About David Moses Bridges

David Moses Bridges, who passed quietly away on January 20, 2017, was a Native American artist who received national recognition for his work—which ranged from Wabanaki birch bark canoes and birch bark containers—using traditional construction techniques. His canoes and baskets are in museums across Maine and throughout the country. Highly regarded in his field, David won numerous awards and worked with a number of museums and cultural institutions, including the Smithsonian Institution and the Abbe Museum in Bar Harbor, Maine, as a researcher, consultant, and educator. David believed that to make baskets and build canoes you needed to know, love, and protect the forest and the land.

David married a Bolivian woman, Patricia Ayala Rocabado, and together had two boys, Sabattus and Natanis, younger brothers to Tobias. At David's funeral, a former Passamaquoddy Chief commented that David was now, "paddling to the stars." Tobias, together with master canoe maker Steve Cayard, who first taught David, built a birch bark canoe in memory of this remarkable man. Tobias used the tools of his great-great-grandfather.

About the Authors

Jean Flahive has written three children's books. She is the author of *The Old Mainer and the Sea* and the coauthor of both *Remember Me: Tomah Joseph's Gift to Franklin Roosevelt,* which won a 2009 Moonbeam Gold Award, and *The Galloping Horses of Willowbrook,* which was a finalist in the 2012 Maine Literary Awards. She is also the author of two young adult historical novels, *Billy Boy: The Sunday Soldier of the 17th Maine* and *Railroad to the Moon: Elijah's Story.* Jean and her husband live on the coast of Maine.

Donald Soctomah is the Passamaquoddy Tribal Historic Preservation Officer and has been on a quest to follow his great-grandfather's footsteps by storytelling and carrying on the traditions of the tribe. He has authored several tribal history books covering the years 1800 to 1950 and two children's books, *Remember Me,* with Jean Flahive, and *Tihtiyas and Jean,* with Natalie Gagnon, which won the iParenting Media Award in Canada. In 2015 Donald was presented with the Lifetime Cultural Achievement Award in Washington, DC, and the Constance Carlson Public Humanities Award in Maine.

About the Illustrator

Mari Dieumegard is the illustrator for the children's book *The Old Mainer and the Sea.* Mari was born and raised in Alaska but now lives with her husband and two children on a pond in Windham, Maine. She is a graduate of the Maine College of Art with a BFA in Painting. Her work can be found in personal collections across the United States and at MariDieumegardArt.com.

Following is the phonetic pronunciation for the Native American names of the birds of the forest. The *audio* Passamaquoddy-Maliseet Dictionary is available at: www.pmportal.org.

mociyehs – partridge
(Muh gee ass)

cihpolakon – eagle
(Cheep lug un)

kuhkukhahs – owl
(Goo goo hahs)

kasq – crane
(Gus q)

tihtiyas – bluejay
(Dee dee yaz)

alamossit – humming bird
(Ul am us id)